EMMANUEL JOSEPH

Global Guardians, Advancing Ethical Business Practices and Environmental Stewardship

Copyright © 2025 by Emmanuel Joseph

All rights reserved. No part of this publication may be reproduced, stored or transmitted in any form or by any means, electronic, mechanical, photocopying, recording, scanning, or otherwise without written permission from the publisher. It is illegal to copy this book, post it to a website, or distribute it by any other means without permission.

First edition

This book was professionally typeset on Reedsy.
Find out more at reedsy.com

Contents

1. Chapter 1: Understanding Ethical Business Practices — 1
2. Chapter 2: The Evolution of Corporate Social Responsibility — 3
3. Chapter 3: Environmental Stewardship: A Business Imperative — 5
4. Chapter 4: Sustainable Supply Chain Management — 7
5. Chapter 5: Innovations in Green Technologies — 9
6. Chapter 6: Employee Engagement and Corporate Culture — 11
7. Chapter 7: The Role of Leadership in Ethical and Sustainable... — 13
8. Chapter 8: Ethical Marketing and Consumer Relations — 15
9. Chapter 9: Community Engagement and Social Impact — 17
10. Chapter 10: Measuring and Reporting Sustainability... — 19
11. Chapter 11: The Global Regulatory Landscape — 21
12. Chapter 12: The Business Case for Sustainability — 24
13. Chapter 13: Challenges and Barriers to Ethical and... — 26
14. Chapter 14: Case Studies of Ethical and Sustainable... — 28
15. Chapter 15: The Future of Ethical Business Practices and... — 30

1

Chapter 1: Understanding Ethical Business Practices

Ethical business practices form the foundation of a sustainable and just global economy. Companies that prioritize ethical conduct in their operations build trust with stakeholders, from employees to consumers. It is essential to recognize the role of corporate governance, transparency, and accountability in promoting ethical behavior. Furthermore, integrating ethical considerations into decision-making processes ensures that businesses not only adhere to legal standards but also uphold the highest moral principles.

Ethical business practices are not just about following laws and regulations but about doing what is right, fair, and just. Companies that prioritize ethics in their operations are more likely to gain the trust and loyalty of their stakeholders. This trust is built through transparency in business dealings, accountability for actions, and a commitment to fairness and integrity. By embedding ethical considerations into every aspect of their operations, businesses can create a positive impact on society and the environment.

Corporate governance plays a crucial role in fostering ethical business practices. Effective governance structures ensure that companies are accountable to their stakeholders and operate with transparency. This includes establishing clear policies and procedures for decision-making, risk management, and compliance. By fostering a culture of accountability, companies can ensure that ethical behavior is prioritized at all levels of the organization.

Incorporating ethical considerations into business decisions requires a proactive approach. This involves assessing the potential impact of business activities on society and the environment and making choices that prioritize long-term sustainability over short-term gains. By adopting a values-driven approach, companies can create a strong ethical foundation that guides their actions and decisions.

2

Chapter 2: The Evolution of Corporate Social Responsibility

Corporate Social Responsibility (CSR) has evolved from a peripheral concern to a central business strategy. Initially perceived as a marketing tool or a philanthropic effort, CSR now encompasses a company's comprehensive impact on society. Modern CSR initiatives address issues such as fair labor practices, community engagement, and environmental conservation. By embedding CSR into their core values, companies can create long-term value for both their business and the broader community.

The concept of CSR has undergone significant transformation over the years. In its early stages, CSR was often seen as a form of charity or a way for companies to give back to society. However, as awareness of social and environmental issues grew, so did the understanding of CSR's importance. Today, CSR is recognized as a critical component of a company's overall strategy, influencing everything from supply chain management to product development.

Modern CSR initiatives are multifaceted and address a wide range of social and environmental issues. Companies are now expected to go beyond mere compliance with regulations and take proactive steps to create positive social impact. This includes implementing fair labor practices, promoting diversity and inclusion, and supporting community development projects. By adopting a holistic approach to CSR, companies can ensure that their operations benefit society as a whole.

Embedding CSR into a company's core values requires a commitment from leadership and a culture that prioritizes social responsibility. This involves setting clear goals, measuring progress, and holding the organization accountable for its impact. By integrating CSR into their business model, companies can create long-term value for their stakeholders and contribute to a more sustainable and equitable world.

3

Chapter 3: Environmental Stewardship: A Business Imperative

Environmental stewardship is no longer optional but a vital business imperative. The depletion of natural resources, climate change, and pollution demand immediate and sustained action from businesses. Companies must adopt sustainable practices to reduce their environmental footprint and contribute to ecological balance. This includes implementing energy-efficient technologies, minimizing waste, and supporting biodiversity. By prioritizing environmental stewardship, businesses can mitigate risks and enhance their resilience in the face of environmental challenges.

The environmental challenges facing the world today are unprecedented in scale and complexity. Climate change, deforestation, pollution, and loss of biodiversity are just a few of the pressing issues that require urgent action. Businesses, as significant contributors to these problems, have a responsibility to be part of the solution. This means adopting practices that reduce environmental impact and promote sustainability.

Sustainable practices can take many forms, from reducing energy consumption and minimizing waste to investing in renewable energy and supporting conservation efforts. Companies can also play a role in raising awareness about environmental issues and advocating for stronger environmental regulations. By taking a proactive approach to environmental stewardship, businesses can demonstrate their commitment to sustainability and build trust with their stakeholders.

Environmental stewardship is not only about mitigating negative impacts but also about creating positive change. This can involve restoring ecosystems, supporting biodiversity, and promoting sustainable development. Companies that prioritize environmental stewardship can enhance their reputation, attract environmentally conscious consumers, and create long-term value for their business and society.

By adopting a holistic approach to environmental stewardship, businesses can ensure that their operations contribute to a sustainable future. This involves integrating environmental considerations into every aspect of their operations, from product design and manufacturing to supply chain management and marketing. By making sustainability a core part of their business strategy, companies can create a positive impact on the environment and society.

4

Chapter 4: Sustainable Supply Chain Management

A sustainable supply chain is crucial for ensuring that business operations do not harm the environment or exploit vulnerable populations. This involves scrutinizing every stage of the supply chain, from sourcing raw materials to delivering the final product. Companies must collaborate with suppliers who share their commitment to ethical and sustainable practices. Transparency and traceability are key components of a sustainable supply chain, allowing businesses to identify and address potential issues proactively.

Sustainable supply chain management involves assessing the environmental and social impact of every stage of the supply chain. This includes evaluating the sustainability of raw materials, the environmental impact of production processes, and the working conditions of employees. Companies must also consider the carbon footprint of transportation and distribution and take steps to minimize waste and energy consumption.

Collaboration with suppliers is essential for achieving sustainability in the supply chain. Companies must work closely with their suppliers to ensure that they adhere to ethical and sustainable practices. This can involve providing training and support, conducting audits, and establishing clear expectations and standards. By building strong relationships with suppliers, companies can ensure that their entire supply chain operates in a sustainable and ethical manner.

Transparency and traceability are key components of a sustainable supply chain. Companies must be able to track the origin of their raw materials and the environmental and social impact of their production processes. This requires robust systems for monitoring and reporting, as well as a commitment to openness and accountability. By providing stakeholders with clear and accurate information about their supply chain, companies can build trust and demonstrate their commitment to sustainability.

Achieving a sustainable supply chain requires a long-term commitment and a willingness to invest in sustainable practices. Companies must continuously assess and improve their supply chain processes, seeking out new opportunities for sustainability and addressing any challenges that arise. By making sustainability a priority in their supply chain management, companies can create a positive impact on the environment and society.

5

Chapter 5: Innovations in Green Technologies

Advancements in green technologies are transforming how businesses operate and contribute to environmental conservation. Renewable energy sources, such as solar and wind power, are becoming more accessible and affordable. Innovations in waste management, recycling, and sustainable agriculture offer new opportunities for reducing environmental impact. Companies that invest in green technologies not only benefit the planet but also gain a competitive edge in the market.

Green technologies are at the forefront of efforts to address environmental challenges. Renewable energy sources, such as solar, wind, and hydropower, are becoming increasingly cost-effective and widely adopted. These technologies offer a sustainable alternative to fossil fuels, reducing greenhouse gas emissions and mitigating climate change. Companies that invest in renewable energy can reduce their carbon footprint and enhance their sustainability credentials.

Innovations in waste management and recycling are also playing a crucial role in environmental conservation. Advanced recycling technologies can recover valuable materials from waste, reducing the need for virgin resources and minimizing landfill use. Companies can also adopt circular economy principles, designing products for reuse and recycling, and promoting sustainable consumption patterns. By embracing these innovations, businesses can reduce waste and create a more sustainable future.

Sustainable agriculture is another area where green technologies are making a significant impact. Precision farming, for example, uses advanced technologies to optimize resource use and minimize environmental impact. This includes using sensors and data analytics to monitor soil health, water use, and crop performance. Sustainable agriculture practices can also involve reducing pesticide and fertilizer use, promoting biodiversity, and supporting regenerative farming techniques. Companies that invest in sustainable agriculture can contribute to food security and environmental sustainability.

In addition to environmental benefits, green technologies offer significant business advantages. Companies that adopt sustainable practices can reduce costs, enhance their reputation, and gain a competitive edge in the market. Consumers are increasingly seeking out environmentally responsible products and services, and businesses that prioritize sustainability can meet this demand. By investing in green technologies, companies can create long-term value for their business and contribute to a sustainable future.

6

Chapter 6: Employee Engagement and Corporate Culture

Employee engagement is a critical factor in driving ethical business practices and environmental stewardship. A company's corporate culture must reflect its commitment to these values, encouraging employees to act as ambassadors of sustainability. This involves providing education and training on ethical and environmental issues, as well as creating opportunities for employees to participate in sustainability initiatives. A motivated and informed workforce can drive significant positive change within an organization.

Creating a corporate culture that prioritizes ethical business practices and environmental stewardship requires a commitment from leadership. Leaders must demonstrate their commitment to these values through their actions and decisions, setting a positive example for employees to follow. This includes establishing clear goals and expectations, providing resources and support, and fostering a culture of transparency and accountability.

Education and training are essential for engaging employees in sustainability efforts. Companies must provide ongoing education on ethical and environmental issues, helping employees understand the importance of these values and how they can contribute. This can involve workshops, seminars, and online courses, as well as opportunities for employees to participate in education and training programs. By providing employees with the knowledge and skills they need, companies can empower them to act as ambassadors of sustainability within the organization and beyond.

Creating opportunities for employees to participate in sustainability initiatives is another key aspect of fostering engagement. This can involve organizing volunteer activities, supporting employee-led sustainability projects, and recognizing and rewarding employees who demonstrate a commitment to ethical and environmental practices. By involving employees in sustainability efforts, companies can create a sense of ownership and pride, motivating them to contribute to the company's goals.

A motivated and engaged workforce can drive significant positive change within an organization. Employees who are committed to ethical business practices and environmental stewardship are more likely to identify and address potential issues, innovate and improve processes, and advocate for sustainability within their teams. By fostering a culture of engagement, companies can harness the collective power of their workforce to achieve their sustainability goals.

7

Chapter 7: The Role of Leadership in Ethical and Sustainable Business

Leadership plays a pivotal role in shaping a company's approach to ethics and sustainability. Leaders must demonstrate a genuine commitment to these principles through their actions and decisions. This involves setting clear goals, establishing accountability mechanisms, and fostering a culture of transparency and integrity. Effective leadership inspires employees and stakeholders to align with the company's vision and contribute to its sustainability efforts.

Leaders set the tone for ethical and sustainable business practices by modeling the behavior they expect from others. This means consistently making decisions that prioritize ethics and sustainability, even when faced with challenges or trade-offs. By demonstrating a commitment to these values, leaders can build trust and credibility with their employees, customers, and other stakeholders.

Setting clear goals and expectations is essential for driving ethical and sustainable business practices. Leaders must establish measurable objectives and communicate them effectively to the organization. This includes defining key performance indicators (KPIs) related to ethics and sustainability, setting targets, and regularly reviewing progress. By holding themselves and their teams accountable, leaders can ensure that the organization remains focused on achieving its goals.

Fostering a culture of transparency and integrity is another critical aspect of effective leadership. Leaders must create an environment where open communication, honesty, and ethical behavior are valued and encouraged. This involves establishing policies and procedures that promote transparency, such as whistleblower protection and regular reporting on sustainability performance. By fostering a culture of integrity, leaders can build a strong ethical foundation for the organization.

Effective leadership also involves engaging with stakeholders and building partnerships to support sustainability efforts. This includes collaborating with industry peers, government agencies, non-governmental organizations, and other stakeholders to address shared challenges and advance common goals. By building a network of support, leaders can amplify their impact and drive meaningful change.

8

Chapter 8: Ethical Marketing and Consumer Relations

Ethical marketing practices are essential for building trust and credibility with consumers. Companies must ensure that their marketing messages are truthful, transparent, and aligned with their values. This includes avoiding misleading claims, respecting consumer privacy, and promoting products that are safe and environmentally friendly. By prioritizing ethical marketing, businesses can build lasting relationships with consumers and enhance their brand reputation.

Truthfulness is a fundamental principle of ethical marketing. Companies must ensure that their advertising and promotional materials accurately represent their products and services. This means avoiding exaggerated or false claims and providing clear and accurate information about product benefits and potential risks. By being honest and transparent in their marketing, companies can build trust with consumers and avoid the negative consequences of misleading advertising.

Respecting consumer privacy is another critical aspect of ethical marketing. Companies must handle consumer data with care and adhere to privacy regulations and best practices. This includes obtaining consent for data collection, being transparent about how data is used, and implementing robust security measures to protect consumer information. By prioritizing consumer privacy, companies can build trust and demonstrate their commitment to ethical business practices.

Promoting products that are safe and environmentally friendly is also essential for ethical marketing. Companies must ensure that their products meet safety standards and do not pose harm to consumers or the environment. This includes sourcing sustainable materials, minimizing the use of harmful chemicals, and reducing the environmental impact of production processes. By promoting sustainable and safe products, companies can align their marketing with their commitment to environmental stewardship.

Building lasting relationships with consumers requires a commitment to ethical marketing practices. Companies must listen to consumer feedback, address concerns, and continuously improve their products and services. This involves engaging with consumers through various channels, such as social media, customer service, and community events. By fostering open and transparent communication, companies can build strong relationships with consumers and enhance their brand reputation.

9

Chapter 9: Community Engagement and Social Impact

Businesses have a responsibility to contribute positively to the communities in which they operate. Community engagement initiatives, such as volunteering, charitable giving, and partnerships with local organizations, can create meaningful social impact. Companies must also address systemic issues, such as inequality and access to education, through targeted programs and investments. By fostering strong community ties, businesses can create a supportive environment for their operations and drive social progress.

Community engagement involves building strong relationships with local communities and addressing their needs and concerns. This can involve supporting local initiatives, such as education programs, health services, and infrastructure development. By investing in the well-being of the community, companies can create a positive social impact and build trust with local stakeholders.

Volunteering and charitable giving are also important aspects of community engagement. Companies can encourage employees to volunteer their time and skills to support local organizations and causes. This can involve organizing volunteer events, providing paid time off for volunteering, and matching employee donations to charitable organizations. By promoting a culture of giving back, companies can demonstrate their commitment to social responsibility and create a positive impact in the community.

Addressing systemic issues, such as inequality and access to education, requires a long-term commitment and targeted investments. Companies can develop programs and partnerships to support underserved populations and create opportunities for social and economic advancement. This can involve providing scholarships, funding job training programs, and supporting initiatives that promote diversity and inclusion. By addressing these systemic issues, companies can contribute to a more equitable and just society.

Building strong community ties involves ongoing engagement and collaboration with local stakeholders. Companies must listen to the needs and concerns of the community and work together to find solutions. This can involve participating in community forums, conducting surveys, and partnering with local organizations. By fostering open and transparent communication, companies can build trust and create a supportive environment for their operations.

10

Chapter 10: Measuring and Reporting Sustainability Performance

Measuring and reporting on sustainability performance is crucial for accountability and continuous improvement. Companies must establish clear metrics and benchmarks to assess their progress towards ethical and environmental goals. Transparent reporting practices, such as sustainability reports and third-party audits, provide stakeholders with the information they need to evaluate a company's performance. This transparency fosters trust and encourages businesses to strive for higher standards.

Establishing clear metrics and benchmarks is the first step in measuring sustainability performance. Companies must define key performance indicators (KPIs) related to their ethical and environmental goals. These KPIs should be specific, measurable, achievable, relevant, and time-bound (SMART). By setting clear targets, companies can track their progress and identify areas for improvement.

Regular monitoring and assessment are essential for measuring sustainability performance. Companies must collect data on their KPIs and analyze it to evaluate their progress. This involves using tools and technologies to track performance, such as sustainability software and data analytics platforms. By continuously monitoring their performance, companies can identify trends, assess the effectiveness of their initiatives, and make data-driven decisions.

Transparent reporting practices are critical for building trust with stakeholders. Companies must communicate their sustainability performance through regular reports, such as annual sustainability reports and corporate social responsibility (CSR) reports. These reports should provide a comprehensive overview of the company's progress towards its ethical and environmental goals, including successes, challenges, and areas for improvement. By providing transparent and accurate information, companies can demonstrate their commitment to accountability and continuous improvement.

Third-party audits and certifications can enhance the credibility of sustainability reporting. Companies can engage independent auditors to review their performance and verify their data. This can involve obtaining certifications from recognized organizations, such as the Global Reporting Initiative (GRI), the Carbon Trust, and the Forest Stewardship Council (FSC). By obtaining third-party verification, companies can provide stakeholders with confidence in the accuracy and reliability of their reports.

11

Chapter 11: The Global Regulatory Landscape

The global regulatory landscape for ethical business practices and environmental stewardship is constantly evolving. Companies must stay informed about relevant laws and regulations in the countries where they operate. Compliance with these regulations is not only a legal requirement but also a demonstration of a company's commitment to ethical conduct. Businesses must also engage with policymakers and industry bodies to advocate for stronger regulations that promote sustainability.

Compliance with relevant laws and regulations is a fundamental aspect of ethical business practices. Companies must stay informed about the legal requirements in the countries where they operate and ensure that their operations comply with these regulations. This includes adhering to environmental regulations, labor laws, anti-corruption laws, and other relevant legislation. By complying with legal requirements, companies can avoid legal penalties, protect their reputation, and demonstrate their commitment to ethical conduct.

Engaging with policymakers and industry bodies is another important aspect of navigating the regulatory landscape. Companies can participate in policy discussions, provide feedback on proposed regulations, and advocate for stronger standards that promote sustainability. This can involve joining industry associations, participating in public consultations, and collaborating with other organizations to influence policy decisions. By engaging with policymakers, companies can contribute to the development of regulations that support ethical and sustainable business practices.

Proactive compliance involves going beyond legal requirements to adopt best practices in ethical and environmental conduct. This can involve implementing voluntary standards, such as the United Nations Global Compact, the International Labour Organization (ILO) conventions, and the ISO 14001 environmental management standard. By adopting these best practices, companies can demonstrate their commitment to sustainability and set an example for others to follow.

Staying informed about the regulatory landscape requires ongoing monitoring and adaptation. Companies must regularly review changes in laws and regulations and assess their impact on their operations. This can involve establishing compliance management systems, conducting regular audits, and providing training to employees on regulatory requirements. By staying informed and proactive, companies can navigate the regulatory landscape effectively and ensure that their operations remain compliant with evolving regulations.

Proactive compliance involves going beyond legal requirements to adopt best practices in ethical and environmental conduct. This can involve implementing voluntary standards, such as the United Nations Global Compact, the International Labour Organization (ILO) conventions, and the ISO 14001 environmental management standard. By adopting these best practices, companies can demonstrate their commitment to sustainability and set an example for others to follow.

Staying informed about the regulatory landscape requires ongoing monitoring and adaptation. Companies must regularly review changes in laws and regulations and assess their impact on their operations. This can involve establishing compliance management systems, conducting regular audits, and providing training to employees on regulatory requirements. By staying informed and proactive, companies can navigate the regulatory landscape effectively and ensure that their operations remain compliant with evolving

CHAPTER 11: THE GLOBAL REGULATORY LANDSCAPE

regulations.

12

Chapter 12: The Business Case for Sustainability

Sustainability is not just a moral obligation but also a strategic business advantage. Companies that embrace ethical and sustainable practices can enhance their brand reputation, attract and retain talent, and access new markets. Additionally, sustainable practices can lead to cost savings through resource efficiency and waste reduction. By integrating sustainability into their business model, companies can create long-term value for themselves and their stakeholders.

One of the key business benefits of sustainability is enhanced brand reputation. Companies that prioritize ethical and sustainable practices are more likely to gain the trust and loyalty of consumers. This can lead to increased sales and market share, as consumers are increasingly seeking out products and services from responsible companies. By aligning their brand with sustainability, companies can differentiate themselves from competitors and create a positive brand image.

Attracting and retaining talent is another significant benefit of sustainability. Employees, especially younger generations, are increasingly looking for employers that align with their values. Companies that demonstrate a commitment to sustainability can attract top talent and reduce employee turnover. This can lead to increased productivity and innovation, as

CHAPTER 12: THE BUSINESS CASE FOR SUSTAINABILITY

employees are more motivated and engaged when they feel their work contributes to a greater purpose.

Sustainable practices can also lead to cost savings through resource efficiency and waste reduction. By optimizing energy use, minimizing waste, and improving operational efficiency, companies can reduce their costs and improve their bottom line. This can involve investing in energy-efficient technologies, implementing recycling programs, and adopting lean manufacturing practices. By reducing their environmental impact, companies can also mitigate risks associated with resource scarcity and regulatory compliance.

Integrating sustainability into the business model involves a long-term commitment and strategic planning. Companies must assess their operations, identify opportunities for improvement, and set clear sustainability goals. This requires collaboration across departments and engagement with stakeholders to ensure that sustainability efforts are aligned with the company's overall strategy. By taking a holistic approach to sustainability, companies can create long-term value for themselves and their stakeholders.

13

Chapter 13: Challenges and Barriers to Ethical and Sustainable Practices

Implementing ethical and sustainable practices is not without challenges and barriers. Companies may face resistance from internal and external stakeholders, financial constraints, and operational complexities. It is essential to recognize these challenges and develop strategies to overcome them. This involves fostering a culture of innovation, building partnerships, and leveraging technology to drive change. By addressing these barriers, businesses can pave the way for successful implementation of their sustainability initiatives.

Resistance from internal stakeholders can be a significant barrier to implementing ethical and sustainable practices. Employees, managers, and executives may be hesitant to change established processes or invest in new initiatives. This resistance can stem from a lack of understanding, fear of the unknown, or concerns about the impact on performance and profitability. To overcome this resistance, companies must engage with stakeholders, provide education and training, and demonstrate the long-term benefits of sustainability.

External stakeholders, such as suppliers, customers, and investors, can also present challenges. Suppliers may be resistant to adopting sustainable practices, customers may be unwilling to pay a premium for sustainable products, and investors may prioritize short-term returns over long-term sustainability goals. To address these challenges, companies must build strong relationships with stakeholders, communicate the value of sustainability, and demonstrate the business case for ethical and sustainable practices.

Financial constraints are another common barrier to sustainability. Implementing sustainable practices often requires upfront investments in new technologies, processes, and infrastructure. For many companies, especially small and medium-sized enterprises (SMEs), these costs can be prohibitive. To overcome financial constraints, companies can explore alternative financing options, such as grants, loans, and partnerships. They can also prioritize high-impact, low-cost initiatives that deliver quick wins and build momentum for larger investments.

Operational complexities can also pose challenges to implementing sustainability initiatives. This can involve integrating new technologies, reengineering processes, and managing the transition to more sustainable practices. To address these complexities, companies must adopt a systematic approach to change management, involving thorough planning, stakeholder engagement, and continuous monitoring and improvement. By leveraging technology and fostering a culture of innovation, companies can navigate these complexities and drive successful implementation of their sustainability initiatives.

14

Chapter 14: Case Studies of Ethical and Sustainable Companies

Real-world examples of companies that have successfully integrated ethical and sustainable practices provide valuable insights and inspiration. This chapter highlights case studies from various industries, showcasing the strategies and outcomes of leading companies. These case studies demonstrate that ethical and sustainable practices are achievable and beneficial for businesses of all sizes. By learning from these examples, companies can develop their own path towards sustainability.

One example is Patagonia, an outdoor clothing and gear company known for its commitment to environmental and social responsibility. Patagonia has implemented a range of sustainable practices, from using recycled materials in its products to advocating for environmental protection through activism and philanthropy. The company's "Worn Wear" program encourages customers to repair, recycle, and reuse their gear, reducing waste and promoting a circular economy. Patagonia's commitment to sustainability has not only enhanced its brand reputation but also fostered customer loyalty and growth.

Another example is Unilever, a global consumer goods company that has integrated sustainability into its core business strategy. Unilever's Sustainable Living Plan aims to decouple growth from environmental impact and increase positive social impact. The company has set ambitious targets to reduce

CHAPTER 14: CASE STUDIES OF ETHICAL AND SUSTAINABLE...

greenhouse gas emissions, improve water and waste management, and promote sustainable sourcing of raw materials. By embedding sustainability into its business model, Unilever has achieved significant cost savings, enhanced its brand reputation, and driven long-term growth.

IKEA, the Swedish furniture and home goods retailer, is also a leader in sustainability. IKEA has committed to becoming a fully circular and climate-positive business by 2030. This involves designing products for circularity, using renewable and recycled materials, and investing in renewable energy. IKEA's initiatives, such as the "Buy Back" program, encourage customers to return unwanted furniture for refurbishment and resale, reducing waste and promoting a circular economy. The company's commitment to sustainability has strengthened its brand and attracted environmentally conscious consumers.

By examining these case studies, companies can gain valuable insights into the strategies and practices that have led to successful implementation of ethical and sustainable initiatives. These examples demonstrate that sustainability is not only achievable but also beneficial for businesses of all sizes and industries. By learning from the experiences of leading companies, businesses can develop their own path towards sustainability and create long-term value for their stakeholders.

15

Chapter 15: The Future of Ethical Business Practices and Environmental Stewardship

The future of ethical business practices and environmental stewardship is promising, with increasing awareness and commitment from businesses worldwide. Technological advancements, regulatory changes, and shifting consumer preferences will continue to drive progress in this area. Companies must remain proactive and adaptable, constantly seeking new ways to improve their sustainability efforts. By embracing a long-term vision and fostering a culture of innovation, businesses can become true global guardians, advancing ethical practices and environmental stewardship for generations to come.

Technological advancements will play a crucial role in the future of sustainability. Innovations in renewable energy, waste management, and sustainable agriculture will provide new opportunities for businesses to reduce their environmental impact. Companies must stay informed about emerging technologies and explore how they can be integrated into their operations. By investing in research and development, businesses can stay at the forefront of sustainability and drive positive change.

Regulatory changes will also influence the future of ethical business

CHAPTER 15: THE FUTURE OF ETHICAL BUSINESS PRACTICES AND...

practices and environmental stewardship. Governments worldwide are increasingly recognizing the importance of sustainability and implementing stricter regulations to address environmental and social issues. Companies must stay informed about these changes and ensure that their operations comply with new regulations. By engaging with policymakers and advocating for stronger standards, businesses can contribute to the development of regulations that support sustainability.

Shifting consumer preferences will continue to drive demand for ethical and sustainable products and services. Consumers are becoming more conscious of the environmental and social impact of their purchasing decisions and are seeking out companies that align with their values. Businesses must respond to these changing preferences by prioritizing sustainability in their product development, marketing, and operations. By building strong relationships with consumers and demonstrating their commitment to sustainability, companies can enhance their brand reputation and drive long-term growth.

The future of ethical business practices and environmental stewardship requires a long-term vision and a commitment to continuous improvement. Companies must set ambitious goals, measure their progress, and adapt their strategies as needed. This involves fostering a culture of innovation, where employees are encouraged to think creatively and develop new solutions to sustainability challenges. By embracing a long-term vision and fostering a culture of innovation, businesses can become true global guardians, advancing ethical practices and environmental stewardship for generations to come.

Global Guardians: Advancing Ethical Business Practices and Environmental Stewardship

In a world faced with unprecedented challenges, businesses have a crucial role to play in shaping a sustainable future. *Global Guardians* is an inspiring and informative guide that calls on businesses worldwide to embrace their responsibility towards society and the environment. This book delves into the integration of ethical business practices and environmental stewardship, offering insights, strategies, and real-world examples to inspire meaningful change.

Each chapter explores a critical facet of this mission, from understanding the foundations of ethical business practices to the evolution of Corporate Social Responsibility (CSR). Readers will learn about the imperative of environmental stewardship, the importance of sustainable supply chain management, and the transformative potential of green technologies. The book also highlights the significance of employee engagement, leadership, and ethical marketing in driving positive change.

Through detailed case studies, *Global Guardians* showcases companies that have successfully integrated ethical and sustainable practices, providing valuable lessons and inspiration. The book also addresses the challenges and barriers to implementing these practices and offers strategies to overcome them.

Global Guardians is not just a roadmap for businesses but an invitation to join a global movement towards responsible business. By integrating ethical business practices and environmental stewardship, companies can contribute to a more sustainable and equitable future. This book is a call to action for leaders and organizations to become champions of change, advancing ethical practices and environmental stewardship for generations to come. Together, we can create a better world for future generations.

www.ingramcontent.com/pod-product-compliance
Lightning Source LLC
LaVergne TN
LVHW010442070526
838199LV00066B/6148